Animals in the Desert

By John Wood

KidHaven
PUBLISHING

Published in 2018 by
KidHaven Publishing, an Imprint of Greenhaven Publishing, LLC
353 3rd Avenue
Suite 255
New York, NY 10010

Designer: Matt Rumbelow
Editor: Holly Duhig

Cataloging-in-Publication Data

Names: Wood, John.
Title: Animals in the desert / John Wood.
Description: New York : KidHaven Publishing, 2018. | Series: Where animals live | Includes index.
Identifiers: ISBN 9781534523654 (pbk.) | 9781534523630 (library bound) | ISBN 9781534525115 (6 pack) | ISBN 9781534523647 (ebook)
Subjects: LCSH: Desert animals–Juvenile literature.
Classification: LCC QL116.W66 2018 | DDC 591.754–dc23

Printed in the United States of America

CPSIA compliance information: Batch #CW18KL: For further information contact Greenhaven Publishing LLC, New York, New York at 1-844-317-7404.

Please visit our website, www.greenhavenpublishing.com. For a free color catalog of all our high-quality books, call toll free 1-844-317-7404 or fax 1-844-317-7405.

Photo credits: Abbreviations: l-left, r-right, b-bottom, t-top, c-center, m-middle.
Covertr – iFtLizard; Covertm – Francois van Heerden; Covertl – Jacopo Werther; Coverbl – kamon_saejueng; Coverbr – Wolfgang Zwanzger. 2 – Perfect Lazybones. 3: bg – nontthepcool; front – Banana Republic images. 4 – Debbie Steinhausser. 5: bg – smikeymikey1; tl – bikeriderlondon; tr – Ehrman Photographic; m – Banana Republic images; bl – Joe Belanger; br – GUDKOV ANDREY. 6 – Perfect Lazybones. 7 – Jamie Ahmad. 8: bg – Elena Badamshina; tl – Rosalie Kreulen; tr – Villiers Steyn; br – Don Mammoser. 9 – Fotografie-Kuhlmann. 10 – Kris Wiktor. 11 – bierchen. 12 – Peter Barrett. 13 – Alta Oosthuizen. 14 – pixy. 15 – Jason Mintzer. 16 – Matt Jeppson. 17 – Matt Jeppson. 18 – Dmitry Rukhlenko. 19 – Vixit. 20 – LanaElcova. 21 – Ammak. 22 – SeraphP. 23 – Jez Bennett.
Images are courtesy of Shutterstock.com, with thanks to Getty Images, Thinkstock Photo, and iStockphoto.

CONTENTS

Words that look like this can be found in the glossary on page 24.

WHAT IS A HABITAT?

A habitat is a place where an animal lives. It provides the animal with food, shelter, and everything else it needs to survive.

4

There are many different habitats in the world. Each one is home to several different animals.

forests

deserts

grasslands

jungles

oceans

WHAT IS A DESERT?

A desert is a type of habitat that is dry and gets little rain. Deserts can be hot or cold.

Sahara

The biggest cold desert in the world is Antarctica, which is where the South Pole is. The biggest hot desert in the world is the Sahara in Africa.

Antarctica

TYPES OF
DESERT HABITATS

sand dunes

rocky plains

oasis

Hot deserts include many different habitats. Rocky plains, sand dunes, and oases are all homes for desert animals.

Rocky plains are very flat and dusty. Sand dunes are giant hills of sand. Oases are fertile areas in the middle of deserts.

Oases are formed by underground streams that push up through the ground.

ROADRUNNERS

Desert habitats are home to many different animals. The roadrunner is a bird that makes its home in the branches of cactus plants that grow in rocky plains.

The roadrunner can run up to 25 miles (40 kilometers) per hour!

Shown here is a roadrunner eating a lizard.

Rocky plains are home to many lizards, snakes, and spiders, which roadrunners love to eat. This makes rocky plains the perfect home for roadrunners.

MEERKATS

Meerkats like to live in sandy parts of the desert. This is because meerkats make their homes in tunnels under the sand. These tunnels are called burrows.

Shown here is a meerkat on the lookout for danger.

These burrows give the meerkats a place to sleep and look after their young. They also protect the meerkats from predators, such as eagles.

FRINGE-TOED
LIZARDS

Fringe-toed lizards make their homes in sand dunes. Their long toes allow them to move easily through the sand.

Fringe-toed lizards sleep in burrows during the winter months. This is called hibernation. Hibernation protects them from the cold winter weather.

A fringe-toed lizard is shown here warming itself in the sunshine.

15

SHOVELNOSE
SNAKES

Shovelnose snakes also like to live in sand dunes. Their shovel-shaped snouts help them quickly burrow into the sand. This is known as sand swimming.

shovelnose snake

16

To avoid the heat in the desert, the shovelnose snake sleeps during the day. It comes out and hunts at night when it is cooler.

Many snakes are nocturnal.

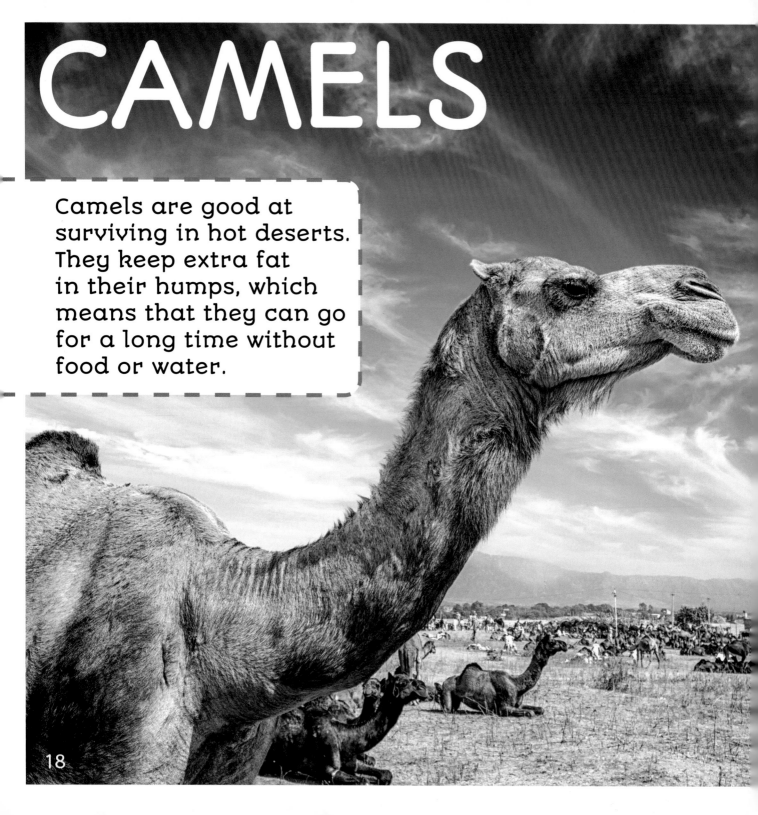

CAMELS

Camels are good at surviving in hot deserts. They keep extra fat in their humps, which means that they can go for a long time without food or water.

People crossing the desert often take camels with them. This is because there is no need to carry extra water for the camels.

People often stop at oases to give their camels a drink.

DESERTS IN
DANGER

When harmful gases from cars, airplanes, and factories go into the air, they trap heat on Earth and cause the planet to warm up. This is called global warming, and it is putting deserts in danger.

We can help slow down global warming by walking short distances instead of using a car.

Global warming can make desert habitats even hotter and drier. This makes it harder for the animals that live in deserts to survive. When an animal is struggling to survive, it is said to be endangered.

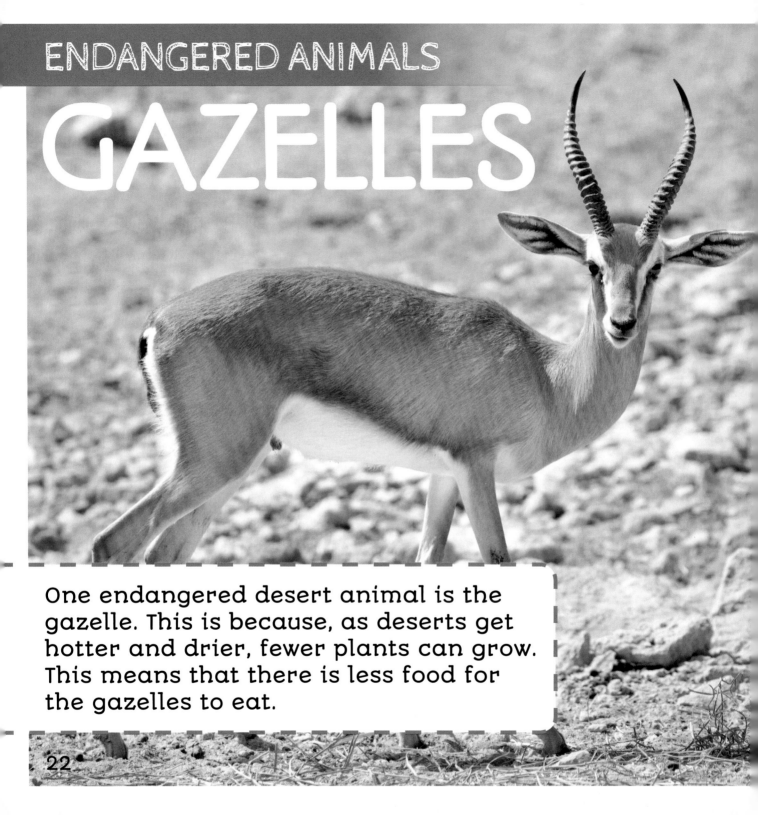

GAZELLES

One endangered desert animal is the gazelle. This is because, as deserts get hotter and drier, fewer plants can grow. This means that there is less food for the gazelles to eat.

AFRICAN WILD DOGS

African wild dogs are endangered because people have built houses and roads in their habitat. This means they have less space to hunt for food.

GLOSSARY

endangered   in danger of dying out

gas   an air-like substance that moves around freely

nocturnal   active at night instead of during the day

predator   an animal that hunts other animals for food

shelter   protection from danger and harsh weather

snout   a nose and mouth that stick out in front of an animal's face

South Pole   the southernmost point on Earth

Index